Why?

Mary Elizabeth Salzmann

Published by SandCastle™, an imprint of ABDO Publishing Company, 4940 Viking Drive, Edina, Minnesota 55435.

Printed in the United States.

Photo credits: Adobe, Corel, Digital Stock, EyeWire, PhotoDisc

Library of Congress Cataloging-in-Publication Data

Salzmann, Mary Elizabeth, 1968-
    Why? / Mary Elizabeth Salzmann.
       p. cm. -- (Do you wonder?)
    Summary: Simple questions and answers about why we do specific things.
    ISBN 1-57765-173-1 (alk. paper) -- ISBN 1-57765-281-9 (set)
       1. Readers (Primary) 2. Readers--Children's questions and answers. [1. Readers.
2. Questions and answers.] I. Title.

PE1119 .S2354 2000
428.6--dc21

              99-046885

The SandCastle concept, content, and reading method have been reviewed and approved by a national advisory board including literacy specialists, librarians, elementary school teachers, early childhood education professionals, and parents.

Let Us Know

After reading the book, SandCastle would like you to tell us your stories about reading. What is your favorite page? Was there something hard that you needed help with? Share the ups and downs of learning to read. We want to hear from you! To get posted on the Abdo Publishing Company Web site, send us email at:

sandcastle@abdopub.com

About SandCastle™
Nonfiction books for the beginning reader

- Basic concepts of phonics are incorporated with integrated language methods of reading instruction. Most words are short, and phrases, letter sounds, and word sounds are repeated.

- Readability is determined by the number of words in each sentence, the number of characters in each word, and word lists based on curriculum frameworks.

- Full-color photography reinforces word meanings and concepts.

- "Words I Can Read" list at the end of each book teaches basic elements of grammar, helps the reader recognize the words in the text, and builds vocabulary.

- Reading levels are indicated by the number of flags on the castle.

Look for more SandCastle books in these three reading levels:

Level 1 (one flag)	Level 2 (two flags)	Level 3 (three flags)

Grades Pre-K to K 5 or fewer words per page	**Grades K to 1** 5 to 10 words per page	**Grades 1 to 2** 10 to 15 words per page

I use the word **why** to ask questions about the reasons for things.

Why do we raise our hands?

We raise our hands because we know the answer.

Why do we wear raincoats?

We wear raincoats to stay dry in the rain.

Why do I like tennis?

I like tennis because it is fun.

Why do I wear sunglasses?

I wear sunglasses because the sun is bright.

Why are we running?

We are running so our kite will fly.

Why are we cheering?

We are cheering because we won the game.

Why do we wear life vests?

We wear life vests to be safe near water.

Why am I sleeping?

I am sleeping because it is nighttime.

Words I Can Read

Nouns

A noun is a person, place, or thing

answer (AN-sur) p. 7
game (GAME) p. 17
kite (KITE) p. 15
nighttime (NITE-time)
  p. 21

rain (RAYN) p. 9
sun (SUHN) p. 13
tennis (TEN-iss) p. 11
water (WAW-tur) p. 19
word (WURD) p. 5

Plural Nouns

A plural noun is more than one
person, place, or thing

hands (HANDZ) p. 7
life vests (LIFE VESTSS)
  p. 19
questions
  (KWESS-chuhnz) p. 5

raincoats (RAYN-kohtss)
  p. 9
reasons (REE-zuhnz) p. 5
sunglasses
  (SUHN-glass-iz) p. 13
things (THINGZ) p. 5

Pronouns

A pronoun is a word that replaces a noun

I (EYE) pp. 5, 11, 13, 21
it (IT) pp. 11, 21

we (WEE) pp. 7, 9, 15, 17, 19

22

Verbs

A verb is an action or being word

am (AM) p. 21
are (AR) pp. 15, 17
ask (ASK) p. 5
be (BEE) p. 19
cheering (CHIHR-ing) p. 17
do (DOO) pp. 7, 9, 11, 13, 19
fly (FLYE) p. 15
is (IZ) pp. 11, 13, 21
know (NOH) p. 7

like (LIKE) p. 11
raise (RAYZ) p. 7
running (RUHN-ing) p. 15
sleeping (SLEEP-ing) p. 21
stay (STAY) p. 9
use (YOOZ) p. 5
wear (WAIR) pp. 9, 13, 19
will (WIL) p. 15
won (WUHN) p. 17

Adjectives

An adjective describes something

bright (BRITE) p. 13
dry (DRYE) p. 9
fun (FUHN) p. 11

our (OUR) pp. 7, 15
safe (SAYF) p. 19

Adverbs

An adverb tells how, when, or where
something happens

why (WYE) pp. 5, 7, 9, 11, 13, 15, 17, 19, 21

23

Glossary

game – an activity with rules that can be played by one or more people.

hands – the parts of your body at the ends of your arms that include your wrist, palm, fingers, and thumbs.

kite – a frame covered with paper or fabric that is attached to a long string and flown in the wind.

life vests – vests filled with air or foam used to keep people afloat in water.

nighttime – the time between sunset and sunrise, when it is dark outside.

sunglasses – dark glasses that protect your eyes from sunlight.

tennis – a game played by two or four players who use rackets to hit a ball over a net.